Iraq

MEL FRIEDMAN

Children's Press®
An Imprint of Scholastic Inc.
New York Toronto London Auckland Sydney
Mexico City New Delhi Hong Kong
Danbury, Connecticut

Content Consultant

Magnus T. Bernhardsson, Ph.D.
Associate Professor of Middle Eastern History
Department of History
Williams College
Williamstown, MA

Library of Congress Cataloging-in-Publication Data

Friedman, Mel, 1946–
  Iraq / by Mel Friedman.
      p. cm. — (A true book)
  Includes index.
  ISBN-13: 978-0-531-16891-2 (lib. bdg.)   978-0-531-21358-2 (pbk.)
  ISBN-10: 0-531-16891-3 (lib. bdg.)   0-531-21358-7 (pbk.)

1. Iraq—Juvenile literature. I. Title. II. Series.

  DS70.62.F75 2009
  956.7—dc22   2008014783

Produced by Weldon Owen Education Inc.

1 2 3 4 5 6 7 8 9 10 R 18 17 16 15 14 13 12 11 10 09   62

Find the Truth!

Everything you are about to read is true *except* for one of the sentences on this page.

Which one is **TRUE**?

T or F   Migrating birds make frequent stopovers in Iraq.

T or F   Ancient Baghdad was built in a perfect square.

Find the answers in this book.

Sacred ibis

Contents

Celil Hayat Mosque

4

In Iraq's deserts, camels can go for more than four days without drinking.

THE **BIG** TRUTH!

Holy Towers

Where the Tigris and Euphrates rivers meet, they form a new river called the Shatt al-Arab.

CHAPTER 1

A Tale of Two Rivers

Iraq covers an area once known as Mesopotamia, or "the land between the rivers." Its two great rivers, the Tigris and Euphrates (yoo-FRAY-teez), supplied water for some of the world's first civilizations. These rivers continue to make life possible in a region that has undergone centuries of change and is still changing today.

For centuries, people living near the two great rivers built houses out of reeds.

Center Stage

Iraq is located in Southwest Asia in a region known as the Middle East. The country is about the size of California. It shares borders with six nations.

Iraq's history has been shaped by its geography. Its famous river valley provided **fertile** farmland in the midst of great deserts. Its location, along the camel paths linking Asia and Europe, made it a key center for trade and culture. Now the country sits on what is believed to be one of the largest oil supplies in the world.

Up until the 1950s, camel trains were used to cross Iraq's large desert. Today, trucks are more common.

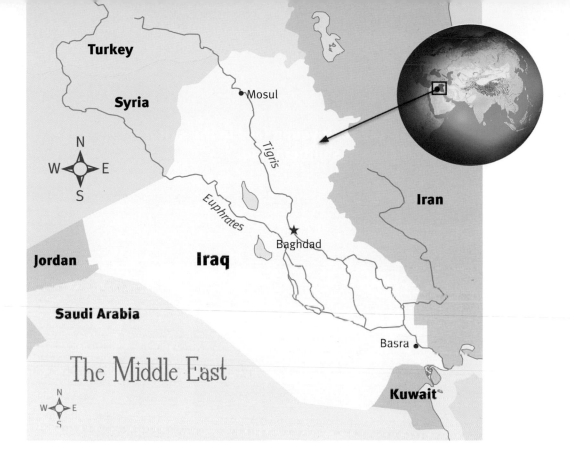

The Middle East

Iraq's location has also contributed to its long history of war. Ancient conquerors came from all sides to claim the land. More recently, wars with neighboring countries expanded to involve distant nations. Today, Iraqis struggle to find peace and make the most of their rich resources.

Greater flamingos and their young feed in the salty lakes and marshlands of southern Iraq.

CHAPTER 2

Desert, Mountains, and Marshes

 Iraq is an important rest stop for birds migrating between Asia and Europe.

Almost one-third of Iraq is made up of flat desert plains. Most Iraqis live close to the rivers in the Tigris-Euphrates Valley. The two rivers merge in southern Iraq. Flooding in this area creates marshes in which date palms thrive. These wetlands are also havens for many types of birds.

In the mountains of Iraq, farmers may live in small villages where the houses are made from dried mud.

Rugged Landscapes

Iraq's desert is home to **nomads**, known as Bedouins (BEH-doo-ihnz), who are animal herders. Dry riverbeds run through parts of the desert. These are called wadis (WAH-deez). During the rare times it rains in the desert, wadis can suddenly flood. Northern Iraq has rolling plains, snowy mountains, and Iraq's only forests. In winter, the plains get enough rainfall for crops and wild plants to grow.

Animal Life

Iraq has wild animals, such as camels and jackals, that can survive in the desert. Gazelles, foxes, and wild pigs live on the plains or in the forests. Ducks, herons, and many other birds are at home on the marshes. At one time, lions and a kind of antelope called an oryx (AWR-iks) were common in Iraq. Now they are extinct there.

Arabian horses originally came from Iraq and other areas of the Middle East. Today this breed can be found around the world.

From Farming to Factories

Many Iraqis depend on agriculture for their living. Iraq's main crops are dates, wheat, barley, and rice. Farmers raise cattle, goats, and sheep. In recent years, Iraqis have been moving from the country to cities to work in industries. Iraq's main industries are petroleum **refining** and chemical manufacturing. There are also factories making textiles, cement, iron, and steel.

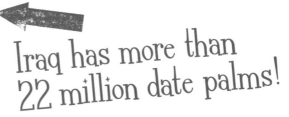

Iraq has more than 22 million date palms!

Farmers climb tall date palms to harvest the fruit.

14

Control Over Oil

In 1927, a mostly British-owned company struck oil in northern Iraq—lots of oil. For nearly 50 years, foreign companies controlled Iraq's oil industry and much of its wealth. The Iraqi government took over these companies in 1975. Oil became Iraq's most valuable source of income. Today, the nation's oil industry is working to recover from three damaging wars that the country has fought since 1980.

Some oil tanks were set on fire by Iraqis when U.S. forces invaded Iraq in 2003.

This panel is one of the treasures from the tombs of Ur. It shows armies going to war.

Changing Governments

 Gold, jewels, and other treasures were found in the tombs of the ancient city of Ur, near Baghdad.

In about 3500 B.C.E., a people known as the Sumerians (soo-MAIR-ee-uhnz) lived in Mesopotamia. They created the world's first civilization. They built the first cities, invented wheeled vehicles, and developed the first known writing system. Since then, many other peoples have invaded and controlled the land that is now called Iraq.

String of Kings

In 2334 B.C.E., a king named Sargon established the world's first empire in Mesopotamia. Persians from the east invaded the area in 539 B.C.E. They came from the land that is now Iran. Two hundred years later, the Greeks defeated the Persians. A Greek king, Alexander the Great, planned to make the great city-state of Babylon the "capital of the world." But after his death, **rival** groups fought for control of the land.

A Mesopotamian king named Hammurabi created one of the world's first written sets of laws. In about 1750 B.C.E., the laws were carved into stone slabs that were decorated with these figures.

Islamic mosques, such as this one in the city of Najaf, often feature domes, towers called minarets, and colorful tiles.

A New Religion

In 622 C.E., a powerful new force arose in the region. Armies from the Arabian Peninsula swept across the Middle East in search of a new religion called Islam. In 762, Baghdad became the capital of a vast Islamic empire. The city was built in a perfect circle on Babylonian ruins. Arabic became Iraq's main language and Islam its main religion.

Battles over Baghdad

In the 1530s, Baghdad was seized by the Ottoman Empire. The Ottomans came from what is now Turkey. They ruled until the end of World War I (1914–1918). After the war, Great Britain took over and created a new country from three Ottoman territories: Baghdad, Basra, and Mosul. The British chose a king to rule Iraq. His name was King Faysal.

In 1958, army officers overthrew the third and last Iraqi king. The officers struggled for power. In 1979, an officer named Saddam Hussein emerged victorious. He became the first president of Iraq.

Time Line of Iraq

750

Arabs create a huge Islamic empire stretching from Spain, through the Middle East, to India.

1500s

Led by Süleyman the Magnificent, Turkey takes control of Iraq, as part of its Ottoman Empire.

Hussein ruled as a **dictator**. In 1980, he started a bloody and costly eight-year war with a neighboring country, Iran. Two years after the war ended, Hussein invaded Kuwait. In 1991, a group of nations led by the United States entered the war and forced the Iraqis out of Kuwait.

The agreement that ended the war allowed the United Nations to check for illegal **weapons of mass destruction**. But Saddam Hussein's government repeatedly tried to keep out the weapons inspectors.

1932
Iraq becomes an independent country under King Faysal I.

2005
On October 15, 2005, Iraqi citizens vote to approve a new constitution.

After the war, U.S. troops helped to pull down statues of Saddam Hussein.

In 2003, the United States, Great Britain, and other allies invaded Iraq. Their goals were to remove Hussein from power and destroy illegal weapons. Officially, the war was over in weeks. However, the fighting continued for years. Hussein was captured and later executed. No weapons of mass destruction were ever found.

Finding Peace

After the fall of Saddam Hussein, the task of setting Iraq on a stable course was difficult. The economy was in ruins. There was a lot of violence between different **ethnic** and religious groups. In 2008, high levels of U.S. troops were still in the country.

A U.S. soldier greets children in Baghdad while on patrol in 2008.

This winged figure once stood on the gates to a city in Mesopotamia. The pinecone in his right hand is a symbol of blessing and protection.

CHAPTER 4

Mother of Inventions

Iraq was the birthplace of some of the world's most important inventions. The ancient Mesopotamians gave us the 60-second minute and the 60-minute hour. They developed the first accurate calendar, the first maps, and the first schools.

The Mesopotamians created the signs of the zodiac by grouping stars into 12 sections.

Writing was first used to keep track of goods sold or stored. A tally of sheep, for example, could be made on a tablet.

Signs of the Times

The oldest known writing system developed in Mesopotamia around 3200 B.C.E. It is called cuneiform (KYOO-nee-uh-form). This script used about 600 signs instead of an alphabet. Each sign stood for a word or a syllable. Signs were written by pressing a reed into soft clay tablets.

Writing was used for keeping records. By about 2000 B.C.E., it was also used for writing stories and poems. The legend of Gilgamesh, the world's first written story, was engraved on several stone tablets. It tells the tale of a Sumerian who was part god and part human.

Great Architecture

Iraq is known for its magnificent architecture. According to legend, Mesopotamia was home to the Hanging Gardens of Babylon. These were lush gardens built high off the ground. They were considered one of the Seven Wonders of the Ancient World. Many beautiful mosques were also built during the Golden Age of the Arab Empire. This period lasted from about 750 C.E. to 945 C.E.

The Hanging Gardens of Babylon were said to have been built about 600 B.C.E. by Babylonian King Nebuchadnezzar (nehb-uh-kuhd-NEHZ-uhr).

Big on Books

During the Golden Age, Arab **scholars** discovered the works of ancient Greek scientists and **philosophers**. It had been thought that these works were lost. However, Arabic translations of them had been preserved. Scholars in Baghdad translated the books into Latin, the scholarly language of Europe. These translations proved important to future philosophers and scientists.

A collection of stories called *The Thousand and One Nights* was written during the Golden Age of the Arab Empire. This illustration from a modern version of the book is from a story called *Ali Baba and the Forty Thieves*.

28

The oud is a very old instrument. Instruments that look like it can be seen in Mesopotamian art.

Unusual Instruments

Modern Iraqi music draws upon three cultures —Arab, Persian, and Turkish. *Maqamat* is one popular form of Arab classical music. High-pitched singing is accompanied by violins, drums, and an oud, a pear-shaped stringed instrument. Bedouin songs are popular in **rural** areas. They are often performed on a *rebab*. This instrument is similar to a fiddle with a single string.

The rebab spread from Africa to the Middle East, over many centuries. It is made from wood and animal hide.

29

Holy Towers

Early Mesopotamian cities were built around temples. These temples sat atop towers called ziggurats. People believed that ziggurats connected heaven and earth. Priests used the temples to perform sacrifices to the gods and to read the stars. There are about 25 known ziggurats in Mesopotamia.

Temple

Brick by Brick

It took millions of bricks to build a ziggurat. There were up to seven levels. Some towers rose 300 feet (90 meters) high.

Ramp

Step Up

Priests reached the temple by means of spiral staircases or ramps on the outside. There were living quarters on the temple grounds for priests and servants.

Most Kurds live in the mountainous areas near Iraq's borders with Turkey, Iran, and Syria. Many herd sheep or cattle for a living.

CHAPTER 5

People of Iraq

While the population of Iraq is largely Arab and Muslim, there are different ethnic and religious groups. The Kurds live in the northeast. They form the second-largest ethnic **minority** in the country. Iraq has been a home to many Christians and Jews. Muslims are divided into two major groups—Shiite (SHEE-ite) and Sunni (SOO-nee). These two groups have had periods of conflict in the Middle East.

Some of Iraq's earliest records describe a mountain people, thought to be the Kurds.

Uneasy Relations

Kurds have lived in the regions of Iraq, Iran, Syria, and Turkey since about 2400 B.C.E. Most Kurds are Sunni Muslims. After World War I, world leaders promised the Kurds a homeland but gave that land to Iraq and other nations instead. Many Kurds continue to fight for independence. In the 1970s, Saddam Hussein's government tried to stop the Kurdish independence movement. Many thousands of Kurds were killed. Today, Iraq's Kurds have regained some of their rights.

International agencies came to the aid of Kurds fleeing Hussein's forces. These Kurdish children pose by a bullet-marked mural of Hussein.

About 90 percent of Muslims in the world are Sunni. But in Iraq they are in the minority.

All Muslims believe in one God, called Allah. Their holy book is called the Qur'an.

Old and New Conflicts

Islam is the national religion of Iraq. The faith was founded by the prophet Muhammad in 622. When Muhammad died, the Sunni Muslims won the battle to lead Islam. Many Shiites were then shut out from positions of power. Today, historical conflicts between Iraq's Shiites and Sunnis, and its Arabs and Kurds, are some of the obstacles to a peaceful, stable Iraq.

A craftsman in Iraq hammers decorative patterns into brass platters.

CHAPTER 6

Life Goes On

Iraq's economy was once based on agriculture. Now, most Iraqis live and work in cities. Exposure to modern life has broken down some traditions. Iraqi life has been further changed by the violence and economic stress caused by decades of war. Yet many Iraqis manage to maintain their daily routines and traditions.

← Outdoor markets are common in Iraq. There are stalls selling food and traditional crafts.

Family First

Everyday life in Iraq centers on the family. The oldest male is the head of the household. He controls the family's property. He makes decisions about the children's education and their future careers. He may even decide whom his children will marry. It is not unusual for parents, grown children and their families, and other relatives to live together under the same roof. This is particularly true in Iraq today, because of the war and resulting poverty.

Houses in poorer parts of Baghdad have no electricity. In summer, families spend time in the courtyard where it is cooler.

An Iraqi family shares a special dawn meal, called *Suhoor*, during the holy month of Ramadan.

Sharing Meals

Iraqi hospitality is legendary. Even when food is scarce, an Iraqi host will feed a guest. Popular meals include stuffed eggplants or peppers and meat and vegetable skewers called kebabs. Dishes made with chickpeas or lentils are typical. Fruits and pastries filled with almonds or dates are common desserts.

Outward Appearance

Traditionally, Iraqi men and women do not display affection in public. Both men and women dress modestly. Men typically wear a long-sleeve robe called a *thawb*, or long-sleeve shirts and long pants. Some women wear an Islamic style of dress: long black robes with scarves to cover their hair. Other women choose to wear modest Western-style clothes.

In Iraq, only children or athletes appear in public in short pants.

Soccer Skills

Soccer, or football, is Iraq's most popular sport. Under the rule of Saddam Hussein, members of the Iraqi national football team were often punished and tortured when they lost matches. In 1996, Iraq was ranked 139th in the world. After 2003, the Iraq team had to play home matches in other countries because of threats by terrorists. The team has improved tremendously. In 2007, Iraq won the AFC (Asian Football Confederation) Asian Cup.

Looking Ahead

More than 20 years of war and economic chaos have taken a toll on Iraqi society. Many Iraqis struggle to make a living and survive. Sometimes children drop out of school to help their families. However, there are signs that conditions are improving. More children are staying in school. In 2007, more than half of all teenagers attended high school. Perhaps this generation of children can grow up to lead a stable, unified nation. ★

Up until the 1990s, Iraq was known for its excellent education system. After the war years, schooling is returning to normal again.

True Statistics

Population of Iraq: About 28 million
Size: 168,754 sq. mi. (437,072 sq. km)
Length of coastline: 36 mi. (58 km)
Main cities: Arbil, Baghdad (capital), Basra, Karbala, Kirkuk, Mosul, Najaf
Percentage of land area that is desert: About 40 percent
Percentage of land area that is suitable for farming: Less than 15 percent
Percentage of adults who can read and write: About 70 percent
Number of chapters and verses in the Qur'an: 114 chapters, more than 6,000 verses

Did you find the truth?

T Migrating birds make frequent stopovers in Iraq.

F Ancient Baghdad was built in a perfect square.

Resources

Books

Augustin, Byron, and Jake Kubena. *Iraq* (Enchantment of the World). New York: Children's Press, 2006.

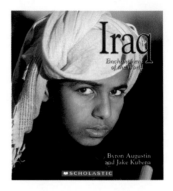

Downing, David. *Iraq: 1968-2003* (Troubled World). Chicago: Raintree, 2004.

Kort, Michael G. *The Handbook of the Middle East*. Minneapolis: Twenty-First Century Books, 2008.

Landau, Elaine. *The Sumerians* (Cradle of Civilization). Brookfield, CT: Millbrook Press, 1997.

Leick, Gwendolyn. *The Babylonian World*. New York: Routledge, 2007.

Malam, John. *Ancient Mesopotamia* (Historic Civilizations). Milwaukee, WI: Gareth Stevens Publishing, 2005.

Ponsford, Simon. *Iraq* (Countries in the News). North Mankato, MN: Smart Apple Media, 2008.

Richie, Jason. *Iraq and the Fall of Saddam Hussein*. Minneapolis, MN: Oliver Press, 2003.

Organizations and Web Sites

Ancient Mesopotamia: This History, Our History

http://mesopotamia.lib.uchicago.edu/

Experience an online archeological dig and explore ancient sites in Iraq.

National Geographic Kids: Iraq

http://kids.nationalgeographic.com/Places/Find/Iraq

Find facts, photos, and a video history of this Middle Eastern civilization.

Write Like a Babylonian

Write your name in cuneiform, the way an ancient Babylonian might have written it.

www.upennmuseum.com/cuneiform.cgi

Places to Visit

The Metropolitan Museum of Art

1000 Fifth Avenue
New York 10028-0198
(212) 535 7710
www.metmuseum.org/
Explore more than 7,000 works of art from the Near East.

The Oriental Institute of the University of Chicago

1155 East 58th Street
Chicago, IL 60637
(773) 702 9514
http://oi.uchicago.edu/museum/meso/
Visit the largest U.S. collection of ancient Iraqi objects.

Important Words

dictator – someone who has complete control of a country, often ruling it unjustly

ethnic – a group of people who share the same national origins, language, or culture

fertile – capable of producing crops; fertile land is good for farming

minority – a population group that is smaller in number than other groups in an area

nomad – a person who moves from place to place

philosopher (fih-LAHS-uh-fer) – a person who studies truth, wisdom, and the nature of reality

refine – to remove unwanted matter from a substance such as oil

rival – competing

rural – having to do with the countryside

scholar (SKOL-ur) – a person who specializes in a particular area of study

weapons of mass destruction – nuclear, biological, or chemical weapons that can inflict serious damage on living and non-living things

Index

Page numbers in **bold** indicate illustrations

About the Author

Mel Friedman is an award-winning journalist and children's book author. He has four graduate degrees from Columbia University, including one in East Asian studies. He also holds a B.A. in history from Lafayette College. He has written or cowritten more than two dozen children's books, both fiction and nonfiction. He speaks and reads Chinese and spent a year in China teaching English at Beijing Normal University's branch campus in Zhuhai, Guangdong Province.